ONE DIRECTION

QUIZ BOOK

By Riley Brooks

SCHOLASTIC

Photo credits

Front cover: © PR Newswire/Associated Press
Back cover: © Ian West/Associated Press

Interior: Page 4: © Yul Mok/Associated Press; Page 5: © Steve Parsons/Associated Press; Pages 6-7: © Dominic Lipinski/Associated Press; Page 9: © Getty Images; Page 13: © IBL/Rex Features/Associated Press; Page 17: © IBL/Rex Features/Associated Press; Page 19: © Newspix via Getty Images; Page 20: © NBCU Photo Bank via Getty Images; Page 21: © Nikki To/Rex Features/Associated Press; Page 23: © IBL/Rex Features/Associated Press; Page 25: © WireImage/Getty Images; Page 26: © John Marshall/Associated Press; Page 27: © Getty Images; Page 30: © IBL/Rex Features/Associated Press; Page 31: © Charles Sykes /Associated Press; Page 33: © IBL/Rex Features/Associated Press; Page 35: © Dominic Lipinski/Associated Press; Page 36: © Yui Mok/Associated Press; Page 37: © Film Magic/Getty Images; Page 38: © Getty Images; Page 41: © Film Magic/Getty Images; Page 43: © Credit Barket/PictureGroup via AP Images; Page 45: © WireImage/Getty Images; Page 47: © WireImage/Getty Images

Vector graphic of fans: © Sabri Deniz Kizil/Shutterstock

© 2012 by Scholastic Inc.
ISBN 978-0-545-50545-1

All rights reserved. Published by Scholastic Inc.
SCHOLASTIC and associated logos are trademarks and/or registered trademarks of Scholastic Inc.

12 11 10 9 8 7 6 5 4 3 2 1   12 13 14 15 16 17/0
Printed in the U.S.A.   40
First printing, September 2012

Table of Contents

The 1D Story

One Direction got their start on the seventh season of the famous UK TV singing competition *The X Factor*. Fans tune in every season to vote as singers compete in four different categories to win a record deal. The categories are boys, girls, over 25-year-olds, or groups.

Liam Payne, Harry Styles, Niall Horan, Louis Tomlinson, and Zayn Malik each had incredible auditions in the boys' category. Niall sang "So Sick," Zayn sang "Let Me Love You," Liam sang "Cry Me a River," Harry sang "Isn't She Lovely," and Louis sang "Hey There Delilah." All five of the guys advanced through several rounds all the way to boot camp, but they were each cut at this round.

Luckily, the story doesn't end there! The judges, including music mogul Simon Cowell, had the brilliant idea that Liam, Harry, Niall, Louis, and Zayn continue through the competition as a boy band. Harry suggested the name *One Direction* for their new group, since all of the boys had the same goal, and, with that, One Direction was born!

1D made it all the way to the final round singing songs like "My Life Would Suck Without You," "Kids in America," and "Chasing Cars." Sadly, One Direction finished in third place, and Matt Cardle took first place. But Simon Cowell was so impressed with the guys that he offered 1D a recording contract with his record label, Syco Records. After a four-month *X Factor* tour, One Direction went straight into the recording studio to create their first album.

Recording an album was everything the boys had dreamed of! "We got lots of say in the album, actually," Liam told irishtimes.com. "We got to choose a lot of the songs and that sort of stuff." The guys even helped with some of the songwriting!

One Direction's first single, "What Makes You Beautiful," was released on September 11, 2011, in the UK and it immediately shot to number one on the UK Singles Chart. 1D followed it up with their second single, "Gotta Be You," on November 11, 2011, and their debut album, *Up All Night*, released a week later on November 18, 2011. It was an instant hit—reaching number two on the UK charts and making the top ten in eighteen other countries.

In the UK, the guys won the 2011 4Music Awards for "Best Group," "Best Breakthrough," and "Best Video," and also beat out Adele to win the 2012 Brit Award for "Best British Single" for "What Makes You Beautiful." They also went on tour all over the United Kingdom, with most shows selling out within minutes.

Next up, One Direction crossed the pond to take on America. The band made history on March 13, 2012, when they released *Up All Night* at number one on the American charts. They were the first British group to ever have a number one debut in the U.S. Harry told cbsnews.com, "It's beyond a dream come true for us."

Quiz #1: How Well Do You Know 1D?

1. All of the One Direction band members are from England except:

   ❑ A. Harry ❑ B. Liam ❑ C. Louis ❑ D. Niall

2. One Direction became a band on this reality TV show:

   ❑ A. *Pop Idol* ❑ B. *The X Factor*
   ❑ C. *Britain's Got Talent* ❑ D. *The Voice*

3. In the reality TV competition where One Direction got their start, 1D came in:

   ❑ A. First place ❑ B. Third place ❑ C. Fifth place ❑ D. Last place

4. This 1D member thought up the name One Direction:

   ❑ A. Liam ❑ B. Zayn ❑ C. Harry ❑ D. Niall

5. The boys of One Direction work with this toy brand:

   ❑ A. Pokémon ❑ B. Bakugan
   ❑ C. Yo Gabba Gabba ❑ D. Scooby-Doo

6. 1D's official Twitter handle is:

   ❑ A. @1D4Ever ❑ B. @onedirection
   ❑ C. @1Direction ❑ D. @1DMusic

7. Which of these singers is not in One Direction?

   ❑ A. Harry Styles ❑ B. Liam Payne
   ❑ C. Louis Tomlinson ❑ D. Matt Cardle

8. The One Direction music video for "Gotta Be You" includes a Volkswagen Beetle in what color?

   ❑ A. Baby blue ❑ B. Bright red
   ❑ C. Lemon yellow ❑ D. Light green

9. One Direction's music video for "One Thing" features the band riding around London in a:

  ❏ A. **Volkswagen Beetle** ❏ B. **Chevy pickup truck**
  ❏ C. **Red double-decker bus** ❏ D. **Mercedes convertible**

10. One Direction's first official single was:

  ❏ A. **"What Makes You Beautiful"** ❏ B. **"Gotta Be You"**
  ❏ C. **"One Thing"** ❏ D. **"More Than This"**

11. 1D set what record in the U.S.?

  ❏ A. **First boy band to have a number one debut in the U.S.**
  ❏ B. **Youngest boy band to have a number one debut in the U.S.**
  ❏ C. **First British group to have a number one debut in the U.S.**
  ❏ D. **Cutest boy band to have a number one debut in the U.S.**

12. The music video for "What Makes You Beautiful" was filmed where?

  ❏ A. **In a forest** ❏ B. **At a mall**
  ❏ C. **On a beach** ❏ D. **In an airplane**

13. 1D is often compared to this 1960s British band:

  ❏ A. **The Beatles** ❏ B. **The Rolling Stones**
  ❏ C. **Herman's Hermits** ❏ D. **The Kinks**

14. The boys of One Direction beat out Adele to win this 2012 Brit Award:

  ❏ A. **Best Breakthrough Artist** ❏ B. **Best Group**
  ❏ C. **Best Music Video** ❏ D. **Best British Single**

15. This TV judge signed 1D to their first record deal:

  ❏ A. **Simon Cowell** ❏ B. **Nicole Scherzinger**
  ❏ C. **Kylie Minogue** ❏ D. **Usher**

Harry Edward Styles was born on February 1, 1994, in Evesham, England, to proud parents Anne and Des. Harry loved singing as a child—especially Elvis Presley's songs. Harry's parents got a divorce when he was seven, but he and his older sister, Gemma, have always been close with both their mom and their dad.

The older Harry got, the more important music became to him. Harry became the lead singer for the band White Eskimo with friends Haydn Morris, Nick Clough, and Will Sweeny at Holmes Chapel Comprehensive School. The group practiced whenever they could and even landed a few gigs at a wedding and some school events after performing at a Battle of the Bands in their town. Luckily, Harry's former bandmates are now his biggest supporters. Harry gained a lot of confidence while performing with White Eskimo, and his charismatic stage style definitely makes him a superstar with One Direction!

STAR STATS

> **Full Name:** Harry Edward Styles

> **Nickname:** Barry

> **Birthday:** February 1, 1994

> **Siblings:** older sister, Gemma

> **Hometown:** Holmes Chapel, England

> **Best Friend:** Louis Tomlinson

> **Favorite Movie:** *Love Actually*

> **Favorite Bands:** Foster the People, Coldplay, Kings of Leon, The Beatles

> **Favorite TV Show:** *Family Guy*

> **Favorite Color:** pink

> **Likes:** Laser Quest

> **Dislikes:** roller coasters, olives

> **Twitter Handle:** @Harry_Styles

Airport Action: A Fill-in-the-Blanks Story

When _____ had to go on a family vacation the
GIRL'S NAME

same week that One Direction was playing in _____, her
NAME OF TOWN

hometown, she was devastated. _____ couldn't believe
SAME GIRL'S NAME

that she was going to miss seeing _____, her favorite
ONE DIRECTION BAND MEMBER

member of 1D! She tried to make the best of the situation—after all,

she was in _____! She put on her _____ and
VACATION SPOT   VACATION OUTFIT

spent plenty of time _____. Soon her vacation was over
VACATION ACTIVITY

and _____ headed back to _____ with her family.
SAME GIRL'S NAME   SAME NAME OF TOWN

When _____ got off the plane, she noticed a
SAME GIRL'S NAME

commotion in the airport. There were _____ and
PLURAL NOUN

reporters everywhere! They all seemed to be looking for something.

_____ pushed her way _____through the crowd
SAME GIRL'S NAME   ADVERB

and, to her surprise, saw the _____ guys of One Direction
ADJECTIVE

walking right toward her! They were on their way to catch their

flight to _____ for their next concert.
EXOTIC DESTINATION

    Just then, the crowd pushed forward and _____
SAME GIRL'S NAME

was knocked _____ to the ground. She landed with a
ADVERB

_____ and cried out. _____ saw her fall and
NOISE   ONE DIRECTION BAND MEMBER

hurried over to help her up, followed by the rest of the band. "I'm

so sorry you fell," _____ exclaimed. "Let me help you."
ONE DIRECTION BAND MEMBER

He pulled _____ to her feet and gave her a big hug.
SAME GIRL'S NAME

    "I'm OK," she answered. "Thanks for your help." He gave her

a/an _____ kiss on the cheek and then hurried off with the
ADJECTIVE

rest of 1D. _____ sighed. It was the _____ end to
SAME GIRL'S NAME   ADJECTIVE

a vacation ever!

Liam James Payne was born to parents Karen and Geoff on August 29, 1993, in Wolverhampton, England. But little Liam had health problems. One of his kidneys wasn't working, so Liam spent most of his childhood in and out of hospitals. Having a great family to support him made all of those doctor's appointments much easier to deal with!

In high school, Liam was one of the stars of his school's cross-country team, and he also took boxing lessons. Liam also had a serious passion for music. He always dreamed of singing, but he was also interested in the business side of the music industry. He studied music technology at the City of Wolverhampton College with plans to look for a behind-the-scenes music job after he graduated. Luckily, Liam never gave up on singing, and auditioned for *The X Factor* twice—once in 2008 and again in 2010, when he landed in One Direction!

STAR STATS

- > Full Name: Liam James Payne
- > Nickname: Ian
- > Birthday: August 29, 1993
- > Siblings: two older sisters, Ruth and Nicola
- > Hometown: Wolverhampton, England
- > Favorite Movie: all 3 Toy Story films
- > Favorite Bands: Two Door Cinema Club, Bing Crosby, John Mayer

- > Favorite Style Product: his pink hair straightener
- > Favorite Color: blue
- > Known As: the "Dad" of One Direction
- > Likes: surprises, aftershave, singing in the shower
- > Dislikes: flying, spoons
- > Twitter Handle: @Real_Liam_Payne

1. The cuties of 1D performed this song at the 2012 *Nickelodeon Kids' Choice Awards:*

   ❏ A. "Up All Night"   ❏ B. "Forever Young"
   ❏ C. "What Makes You Beautiful"   ❏ D. "One Thing"

2. Liam sang this song for his *X Factor* audition:

   ❏ A. "So Sick"   ❏ B. "Let Me Love You"   ❏ C. "Cry Me a River"
   ❏ D. "Hey There Delilah"   ❏ E. "Isn't She Lovely"

3. Harry sang this song for his *X Factor* audition:

   ❏ A. "So Sick"   ❏ B. "Let Me Love You"   ❏ C. "Cry Me a River"
   ❏ D. "Hey There Delilah"   ❏ E. "Isn't She Lovely"

4. Niall sang this song for his *X Factor* audition:

   ❏ A. "So Sick"   ❏ B. "Let Me Love You"   ❏ C. "Cry Me a River"
   ❏ D. "Hey There Delilah"   ❏ E. "Isn't She Lovely"

5. Zayn sang this song for his *X Factor* audition:

   ❏ A. "So Sick"   ❏ B. "Let Me Love You"   ❏ C. "Cry Me a River"
   ❏ D. "Hey There Delilah"   ❏ E. "Isn't She Lovely"

6. Louis sang this song for his *X Factor* audition:

   ❏ A. "So Sick"   ❏ B. "Let Me Love You"   ❏ C. "Cry Me a River"
   ❏ D. "Hey There Delilah"   ❏ E. "Isn't She Lovely"

7. Which of these songs did One Direction not cover on *The X Factor*?

   ❏ A. "My Life Would Suck Without You"   ❏ B. "Chasing Cars"
   ❏ C. "Kids in America"   ❏ D. "Firework"

8. This 1D star was nearly cut from *The X Factor* for not wanting to dance at boot camp:

   ❏ A. Liam   ❏ B. Niall   ❏ C. Harry   ❏ D. Louis   ❏ E. Zayn

9. One Direction's summer 2012 tour takes place in which country?

- ❏ A. England
- ❏ B. Australia
- ❏ C. the United States
- ❏ D. Japan

10. 1D's live performance concert DVD is called:

- ❏ A. *Up All Night: The Live Tour*
- ❏ B. *Forever Young: 1D Live*
- ❏ C. *One Direction Live*
- ❏ D. *A Day with 1D Live*

11. Which fellow *X Factor* contestant is opening for One Direction on their summer 2012 tour?

- ❏ A. Rebecca Ferguson
- ❏ B. Matt Cardle
- ❏ C. Olly Murs
- ❏ D. Jack the Lad Swing

12. What song did 1D record to release if they won *The X Factor*?

- ❏ A. "Up All Night"
- ❏ B. "Forever Young"
- ❏ C. "What Makes You Beautiful"
- ❏ D. "Gotta Be You"

13. 1D starred as the musical guest on this comedy show:

- ❏ A. *Saturday Night Live*
- ❏ B. *Punk'd*
- ❏ C. *So Random!*
- ❏ D. *Off Their Rockers*

14. 1D guest starred and performed on this Nickelodeon TV show:

- ❏ A. *iCarly*
- ❏ B. *Victorious*
- ❏ C. *Supah Ninjas*
- ❏ D. *Fred: The Show*

15. 1D went on tour with this Nickelodeon TV and music star:

- ❏ A. Miranda Cosgrove
- ❏ B. Victoria Justice
- ❏ C. Big Time Rush
- ❏ D. How to Rock

The brown-eyed cutie known as Zayn was born Zain Javadd Malik on January 12, 1993. Zayn is half-Pakistani, by his dad, Yaser, and half-British, from his mom, Tricia. Zayn grew up in West Bowling, England. He and his three sisters got picked on a lot when they were younger because of their mixed heritage. It didn't help that they moved several times and the Malik kids had to change schools.

But Zayn really came into his own when he began school at Tong High School, where he joined his school's theater program. Zayn turned into a charming, charismatic star when he hit the stage. He starred in several of Tong High's musicals, including *Grease*. *The X Factor* took Zayn's love of performing to a new level but he was able to step up to the challenge thanks to his friends and family cheering him on at home!

STAR STATS

> Full Name: **Zain Javadd Malik**

> Nickname: **Wayne, Zayn**

> Birthday: **January 12, 1993**

> Siblings: **sisters Doniya, Waliyha, and Safaa**

> Hometown: **Bradford, England**

> Favorite Movie: *Scarface*

> Favorite Bands: **Usher, Robin Thicke, Michael Jackson, Ne-Yo**

> Favorite Color: **red**

> Bad Habit: **checks himself in every mirror he sees**

> Likes: **scary movies, dancing**

> Dislikes: **crust on sandwiches, swimming**

> Tattoos: **Zayn's grandfather's name in Arabic, a yin yang symbol, the Japanese symbols for "born lucky," and crossed fingers**

> Twitter Handle: **@zaynmalik**

1. *Scarface* is which 1D band member's favorite movie?

   ❑ **A. Liam**   ❑ **B. Niall**   ❑ **C. Harry**   ❑ **D. Louis**   ❑ **E. Zayn**

2. Michael Bublé is which 1D band member's favorite singer?

   ❑ **A. Liam**   ❑ **B. Niall**   ❑ **C. Harry**   ❑ **D. Louis**   ❑ **E. Zayn**

3. *Grease* is the favorite movie of which two 1D band members?

   ❑ **A. Liam and Harry**   ❑ **B. Niall and Louis**
   ❑ **C. Harry and Louis**   ❑ **D. Louis and Zayn**

4. Which 1D band member's favorite TV show is *Family Guy*?

   ❑ **A. Liam**   ❑ **B. Niall**   ❑ **C. Harry**   ❑ **D. Louis**   ❑ **E. Zayn**

5. What is Louis's favorite vegetable?

   ❑ **A. Carrots**   ❑ **B. Broccoli**
   ❑ **C. Celery**   ❑ **D. Cauliflower**

6. Which 1D band member's favorite activity is sunbathing?

   ❑ **A. Liam**   ❑ **B. Niall**   ❑ **C. Harry**   ❑ **D. Louis**   ❑ **E. Zayn**

7. Which 1D band member might you run into playing laser tag?

   ❑ **A. Liam**   ❑ **B. Niall**   ❑ **C. Harry**   ❑ **D. Louis**   ❑ **E. Zayn**

8. Which 1D band member is considered the favorite with female fans?

   ❑ **A. Liam**   ❑ **B. Niall**   ❑ **C. Harry**   ❑ **D. Louis**   ❑ **E. Zayn**

9. Which 1D band member hates olives?

   ❑ **A. Liam**   ❑ **B. Niall**   ❑ **C. Harry**   ❑ **D. Louis**   ❑ **E. Zayn**

10. Which 1D band member hates mayonnaise?

❏ **A.** Liam   ❏ **B.** Niall   ❏ **C.** Harry   ❏ **D.** Louis   ❏ **E.** Zayn

11. Which 1D band member can't swim?

❏ **A.** Liam   ❏ **B.** Niall   ❏ **C.** Harry   ❏ **D.** Louis   ❏ **E.** Zayn

12. Which 1D band member's favorite color is pink?

❏ **A.** Liam   ❏ **B.** Niall   ❏ **C.** Harry   ❏ **D.** Louis   ❏ **E.** Zayn

13. Purple is the favorite color of which 1D band member?

❏ **A.** Liam   ❏ **B.** Niall   ❏ **C.** Harry   ❏ **D.** Louis   ❏ **E.** Zayn

14. Which 1D band member loves surprises?

❏ **A.** Liam   ❏ **B.** Niall   ❏ **C.** Harry   ❏ **D.** Louis   ❏ **E.** Zayn

15. Which 1D band member has a reputation as a practical joker?

❏ **A.** Liam   ❏ **B.** Niall   ❏ **C.** Harry   ❏ **D.** Louis   ❏ **E.** Zayn

All About Louis

Louis William Tomlinson was born on December 24, 1991, in Doncaster, England, to proud parents Johanna and Mark Tomlinson. Louis was joined a few years later by younger sisters Charlotte, Félicité, and then twins, Daisy and Phoebe.

Louis wasn't the first star in the family. As babies, his twin sisters landed a role on *Fat Friends*, a popular British TV show, and Louis got to appear as an extra on the show, too! He also appeared in *If I Had You*, a made-for-TV movie, and on *Waterloo Road*, another British TV show. Louis loved acting and singing, but school was also important to him.

At Hall Cross School, Louis worked hard in his classes and found plenty of time to star in the school's plays and musicals. Louis had never been shy about his dream of being a professional performer, so when he auditioned for *The X Factor* and joined One Direction, no one was surprised!

STAR STATS

- > Full Name: **Louis William Tomlinson**
- > Nickname: **Hughy**
- > Birthday: **December 24, 1991**
- > Siblings: **sisters Charlotte, Félicité, Daisy, and Phoebe**
- > Hometown: **Doncaster, England**
- > Best Friend: **Harry Styles**
- > Favorite Movie: *Grease*

- > Favorite Bands: **Bombay Bicycle Club, The Fray**
- > Favorite Vegetable: **carrots**
- > Favorite Color: **purple**
- > Likes: **sunbathing, silly voices, practical jokes**
- > Dislikes: **not being able to Tweet on planes, being pale**
- > Twitter Handle: **@Louis_Tomlinson**

1D Gets Schooled: A Fill-in-the-Blanks Story

_____ was so worried. She had just been called to the
GIRL'S NAME

principal's _____. She hoped she wasn't in trouble! When
PLACE

she walked through the door, she found her _____ band
ADJECTIVE

One Direction waiting there for her!

"Hi, we're One Direction," _____ said, welcoming
ONE DIRECTION BAND MEMBER

_____ with a big hug. "You've been chosen to keep us
SAME GIRL'S NAME

company before we give a/an _____ concert for your entire
ADJECTIVE

school."

"Wow! That is _____," _____ said.
ADJECTIVE   SAME GIRL'S NAME

"Tell us a little about yourself," _____ said.
DIFFERENT 1D BAND MEMBER

_____ told the guys a little about herself and asked
SAME GIRL'S NAME

them all of the _____ questions she had ever wanted to
ADJECTIVE

know about the band. They told her about the _____ trips
ADJECTIVE

they'd been on and all of the _____ they like. They talked

PLURAL NOUN

for _____ minutes before the principal came back and led

NUMBER

them all to the auditorium for the concert.

When the band hopped on stage, _____ made an

ONE DIRECTION BAND MEMBER

announcement. "We'd like to invite our new friend, _____,

SAME GIRL'S NAME

up on stage with us while we sing '_____.' We just met her

1D SONG

today and she's _____!"

ADJECTIVE

_____ blushed and came up on stage. The guys

SAME GIRL'S NAME

sang directly to her and, at the end of the song, each of them gave

her a hug and a kiss on the cheek. It was the _____ day

ADJECTIVE

_____ had ever had, and she would never forget it as long

SAME GIRL'S NAME

as she lived.

Niall James Horan was born on September 13, 1993, in Ireland. He and his older brother, Greg, were inseparable growing up. Unfortunately, Niall's parents, Maura and Bobby, split up when Niall was five, but they have both always been very supportive of his dreams.

Niall surprised everyone when he started singing out loud in the car one day and his dad and aunt thought the radio was on! It was clear Niall had some serious musical talent, so his family got him a guitar when he was old enough to learn to play.

Niall attended high school at Coláiste Mhuire. He sang and played guitar in a few local concerts and always wowed the crowds. Still, Niall knew that his *X Factor* audition competing against 10,000 other people in his town was the biggest audition of his life! Luckily, Niall never doubted his talent or his dreams—he's now a member of One Direction!

STAR STATS

> **Full Name:** Niall James Horan

> **Nickname:** Kyle

> **Birthday:** September 13, 1993

> **Siblings:** older brother, Greg

> **Hometown:** Mullingar, Ireland

> **Favorite Movie:** *Grease*

> **Favorite Bands:** The Script, Ed Sheeran, Bon Jovi

> **Favorite Singer:** Michael Bublé

> **Favorite Color:** yellow

> **Likes:** soccer

> **Dislikes:** mayonnaise, clowns

> **Twitter Handle:** @NiallOfficial

1. What is Harry's middle name?
    ❏ A. Javadd ❏ B. James ❏ C. Edward ❏ D. William

2. What color are Liam's eyes?
    ❏ A. Brown ❏ B. Blue ❏ C. Green ❏ D. Hazel

3. Who is the only blond in 1D?
    ❏ A. Liam ❏ B. Niall ❏ C. Harry ❏ D. Louis ❏ E. Zayn

4. Which 1D band member's hometown is Mullingar, Ireland?
    ❏ A. Liam ❏ B. Niall ❏ C. Harry ❏ D. Louis ❏ E. Zayn

5. Which 1D band member can't stop checking himself out in mirrors?
    ❏ A. Liam ❏ B. Niall ❏ C. Harry ❏ D. Louis ❏ E. Zayn

6. Which 1D band member can't live without his pink hair straightener?
    ❏ A. Liam ❏ B. Niall ❏ C. Harry ❏ D. Louis ❏ E. Zayn

7. Which 1D band member has told the rest of the band that they can't date his little sisters?
    ❏ A. Liam ❏ B. Niall ❏ C. Harry ❏ D. Louis ❏ E. Zayn

8. Which 1D band member has four tattoos?
    ❏ A. Liam ❏ B. Niall ❏ C. Harry ❏ D. Louis ❏ E. Zayn

9. Which 1D band member is nicknamed Hughy?
    ❏ A. Liam ❏ B. Niall ❏ C. Harry ❏ D. Louis ❏ E. Zayn

10. What is Niall's nickname in the band?
    ❏ A. Kyle ❏ B. Miles ❏ C. Ni-Ni ❏ D. Ireland

11. Which band member was in the band White Eskimo before joining 1D?

❏ **A. Liam** ❏ **B. Niall** ❏ **C. Harry** ❏ **D. Louis** ❏ **E. Zayn**

12. Liam only has one functioning:

❏ **A. Kidney** ❏ **B. Lung** ❏ **C. Big toe** ❏ **D. Ear**

13. Who is the shortest member of 1D?

❏ **A. Liam** ❏ **B. Niall** ❏ **C. Harry** ❏ **D. Louis** ❏ **E. Zayn**

14. This 1D cutie used to take boxing lessons:

❏ **A. Liam** ❏ **B. Niall** ❏ **C. Harry** ❏ **D. Louis** ❏ **E. Zayn**

15. Louis appeared on this TV show as a child:

❏ **A. *The Teletubbies*** ❏ **B. *Fat Friends***
❏ **C. *Britain's Got Talent*** ❏ **D. *In the Night Garden***

The guys of One Direction have made a splash with their good looks, smooth dance moves, and catchy music, but they've also made a big impact when it comes to fashion. Liam, Harry, Zayn, Louis, and Niall have made preppy-cool super chic.

All of the guys love wearing dark jeans, polo shirts, button-down shirts, blazers, and scarves. Of course, each band member makes his own unique style statement as well. Zayn generally chooses baggier pants, snowy white sneakers, and knit caps. Niall loves buttoned-up polo shirts, Henleys, and hoodies, but his blond locks are his signature look! Harry rocks plain T-shirts with cozy sweaters or fashionable blazers, all of which look cute with his tousled curls. Liam is definitely the most low-key member of the group when it comes to fashion. He usually chooses plaid button-down shirts paired with worn-in jeans. Louis is easily the most fashionable member of 1D. He mixes and matches jeans, khakis, and brightly colored pants with sharp blazers, cardigans, and suspenders.

When it comes to awards shows, the guys go all out in modern-cut suits, crisp dress shirts, and skinny ties—making sure they look irresistible on the red carpet! For performances, the guys go for a coordinated look. They usually sport a mix of blazers, cardigans, letter jackets, button-downs, and jeans or khakis. They almost always choose brighter colors when performing to ensure that even their fans in the back row can see them! Of course, for downtime, you can find the guys wearing jeans, T-shirts, and hoodies just like any other regular teen boys. No matter where you spot the guys of 1D, you can be sure that they will always look stylish!

1. 1D has a friendly rivalry with this British boy band:

   ❑ A. J.L.S.
   ❑ B. The Wanted
   ❑ C. McFly
   ❑ D. Boyzone

2. This teen pop sensation visited with 1D in the studio and is in talks to collaborate with the band:

   ❑ A. Joe Jonas
   ❑ B. Cody Simpson
   ❑ C. Justin Bieber
   ❑ D. Nick Jonas

3. The 1D guys met this Nick star when they guest starred on her show:

   ❑ A. Miranda Cosgrove
   ❑ B. Victoria Justice
   ❑ C. Keke Palmer
   ❑ D. Nathalia Ramos

4. This country and pop star is rumored to have a crush on Harry:

   ❑ A. Carrie Underwood
   ❑ B. Kellie Pickler
   ❑ C. Jennette McCurdy
   ❑ D. Taylor Swift

5. Harry couldn't wait to meet this pop star after she told reporters she thought he was a star:

   ❑ A. Beyoncé
   ❑ B. Miley Cyrus
   ❑ C. Rihanna
   ❑ D. Katy Perry

6. Zayn dated this fellow *X Factor* contestant:

   ❑ A. Cher Lloyd
   ❑ B. Rebecca Ferguson
   ❑ C. Pippa Middleton
   ❑ D. Alexandra Burke

7. 1D met this funny Latina when she hosted *SNL* with them:

   ❑ A. Sofia Vergara
   ❑ B. Penelope Cruz
   ❑ C. Salma Hayek
   ❑ D. Selena Gomez

8. This *X Factor* judge and Australian pop princess is still friendly with the 1D boys:

❑ **A. Dani Minogue**　　❑ **B. Kylie Minogue**

❑ **C. Nicole Scherzinger**　　❑ **D. Britney Spears**

9. This British rocker's daughter interviewed the guys on the 2012 *Nickelodeon Kids' Choice Awards* orange carpet:

❑ **A. Peaches Geldof**　　❑ **B. Lily Collins**

❑ **C. Kelly Osbourne**　　❑ **D. Pippa Middleton**

10. The high-school singers on this TV show cover "What Makes You Beautiful" on an episode:

❑ **A. *Jessie***　　❑ **B. *A.N.T. Farm***

❑ **C. *Victorious***　　❑ **D. *Glee***

Mall Mania: A Fill-in-the-Blanks Story

When the guys of One Direction arrived in _____,

YOUR TOWN

they were really _____ to meet their fans at the local mall.

EMOTION

They had a/an _____ surprise set up for one of their fans,

ADJECTIVE

and they couldn't wait to meet her.

All of the fans visiting the mall put their names into a

_____ when they arrived. Then before the autograph

NOUN

signing began, _____ pulled one name out. He announced

1D BAND MEMBER

the winner—it was _____—and invited her to come

YOUR NAME

backstage to have _____ with the band.

FOOD

When _____ walked into the backstage room,

YOUR NAME

the guys were thrilled. _____ was _____!

YOUR NAME   ADJECTIVE

She had on a cool _____ and looked so _____

ARTICLE OF CLOTHING   ADJECTIVE

wearing _____ lipstick. They all sat down to have some

COLOR

_____ and _____, and asked _____
FOOD　　　　　　　　DRINK　　　　　　　　　　　YOUR NAME

all about herself. She told them that she loves _____ and
　　　　　　　　　　　　　　　　　　　　　　　　YOUR FAVORITE HOBBY

_____, and that she wants to be a _____ when
YOUR FAVORITE SUBJECT　　　　　　　　　　　　PROFESSION

she grows up.

　　The boys all thought _____ was _____,
　　　　　　　　　　　　　　YOUR NAME　　　　　　　ADJECTIVE

but _____ especially liked her. He gave _____
YOUR FAVORITE 1D BAND MEMBER　　　　　　　　　　　YOUR NAME

a special gift—a _____ necklace in the shape of a
　　　　　　　　　GEMSTONE

_____. _____ loved it! She gave Liam, Harry,
SHAPE　　　　　　YOUR NAME

Zayn, Niall, and Louis all big hugs, and thanked them for the

_____ surprise. The guys all promised to call her the next
ADJECTIVE

time they were in _____. They were so glad the fan that
　　　　　　　　　YOUR TOWN

won had been so _____. It was an awesome trip to the
　　　　　　　　　ADJECTIVE

_____ mall!
YOUR TOWN

1. Your ideal first date would be:
   - ❏ A. A movie date
   - ❏ B. A trip to the arcade
   - ❏ C. A nice meal out
   - ❏ D. Tickets to a comedy show
   - ❏ E. A total surprise from start to finish

2. You always go for guys with:
   - ❏ A. A great smile
   - ❏ B. Curls
   - ❏ C. Straight, shaggy hair
   - ❏ D. Deep brown eyes
   - ❏ E. Blond hair

3. Your favorite food to share with a date is:
   - ❏ A. Fried chicken
   - ❏ B. Tacos
   - ❏ C. Pizza
   - ❏ D. Dessert
   - ❏ E. Chinese food

4. You can't resist:
   - ❏ A. A short cutie
   - ❏ B. A fashionable guy
   - ❏ C. A star actor
   - ❏ D. An athletic guy
   - ❏ E. A guy who plays guitar

5. You love a guy who rocks:
   - ❏ A. Pure white sneakers
   - ❏ B. A blazer
   - ❏ C. Suspenders
   - ❏ D. Plaid shirts
   - ❏ E. Polo shirts

6. If your date played a practical joke on you, you would:
   - ❏ A. Laugh! He didn't do it in public, so it's all good.
   - ❏ B. Plot a joke to play on him with his best friend.
   - ❏ C. Play one on him to get even.
   - ❏ D. Let him buy you dinner to make up for it.
   - ❏ E. Admit he got you good—you aren't the type to get even.

7. You can't imagine a better way to be asked out than if your crush:

   ❑ A. Challenged you to a dance-off, with the winner picking the activity.

   ❑ B. Winked at you and asked for your number.

   ❑ C. Tweeted you.

   ❑ D. Sang you a song.

   ❑ E. Told you that you were the most beautiful girl he'd ever seen.

8. You would most want to dance with your crush to which song?

   ❑ A. Michael Jackson's "Thriller"

   ❑ B. Coldplay's "Paradise"

   ❑ C. The Fray's "How to Save a Life"

   ❑ D. Bing Crosby's "Waltzing in a Dream"

   ❑ E. Bon Jovi's "Livin' on a Prayer"

9. If your crush took you to a movie, you would pick:

   ❑ A. A scary movie   ❑ B. A romantic comedy   ❑ C. A comedy
   ❑ D. An animated flick   ❑ E. A musical

10. Your perfect movie snack to share with your crush would be:

   ❑ A. Chicken nuggets   ❑ B. Popcorn   ❑ C. Cookie dough
   ❑ D. Chocolate candy   ❑ E. Spring rolls

11. If your crush invited you over for dinner with his family, you'd look forward to:

   ❑ A. Trying out authentic Pakistani food.

   ❑ B. Meeting his former bandmates over dessert.

   ❑ C. Meeting his little sisters.

   ❑ D. A dinner that required no spoons.

   ❑ E. A dish made from real Irish potatoes.

12. Which sporty activity would you like to do with your crush?

   ❑ A. Basketball ❑ B. Tennis ❑ C. Surfing ❑ D. Running ❑ E. Soccer

13. Your favorite 1D singer is:

❏ **A. Zayn** ❏ **B. Harry** ❏ **C. Louis** ❏ **D. Liam** ❏ **E. Niall**

14. If your date brought you your favorite flowers, they would be:

❏ **A. Red roses** ❏ **B. Pink peonies** ❏ **C. Purple irises**
❏ **D. Blue hydrangeas** ❏ **E. Yellow tulips**

Check your answers from all of the quizzes and see just how big a 1D fan you are!

Quiz #1: 1.D 2.B 3.B 4.C 5.A 6.B 7.D 8.A 9.C 10.A 11.C 12.C 13.A 14.D 15.A

Quiz #2: 1.C 2.C 3.E 4.A 5.B 6.D 7.D 8.E 9.C 10.A 11.C 12.B 13.A 14.A 15.C

Quiz #3: 1.E 2.B 3.B 4.C 5.A 6.D 7.C 8.C 9.C 10.B 11.E 12.C 13.D 14.A 15.D

Quiz #4: 1.C 2.A 3.B 4.B 5.E 6.A 7.D 8.E 9.D 10.A 11.C 12.A 13.E 14.A 15.B

Quiz #5: 1.B 2.C 3.A 4.D 5.C 6.B 7.A 8.B 9.C 10.D

Quiz #6: If you answered mostly As, then your 1D match is Zayn. If you answered mostly Bs, then your 1D match is Harry. If you answered mostly Cs, then your 1D match is Louis. If you answered mostly Ds, then your 1D match is Liam. If you answered mostly Es, then your 1D match is Niall.

If you answered most of the questions right, you are a 1D SUPERFAN! You follow the band's Tweets, read every interview the boys give, have seen all of their official music videos, and never miss a TV appearance. If you ever get the chance to meet 1D, the guys will definitely be impressed with your dedication!

If you answered half of the questions right, you are a pretty big 1D fan. You love One Direction's music and you know all the basics. If you ever meet the band, you'll have plenty to talk to the guys about!

If you didn't get many questions right, you may need to brush up on your One Direction facts. After all, you wouldn't want to be unprepared in case you get to meet the 1D cuties in person someday!